KALEIDOSCOPE

Tornadoes

Joe Thoron

Marshall Cavendish
Benchmark
New York

Many thanks to Mike Hudson, Warning Coordination Meteorologist at the Kansas City office of the National Weather Service, for his expert review of the tornado diagram used in this book.

Marshall Cavendish Benchmark
99 White Plains Road
Tarrytown, New York 10591-9001
www.marshallcavendish.us

All Internet sites were available and accurate when sent to press.

Library of Congress Cataloging-in-Publication Data
Thoron, Joe.
Tornadoes / by Joe Thoron.
p. cm. — (Kaleidoscope)
Includes bibliographical references and index.
ISBN-13: 978-0-7614-2104-7
ISBN-10: 0-7614-2104-1
1. Tornadoes—Juvenile literature. I. Title. II. Series: Kaleidoscope (Tarrytown, N.Y.)
QC955.2.T485 2006   551.55'3—dc22   2005023345

Editor: Marilyn Mark
Editorial Director: Michelle Bisson
Art Director: Anahid Hamparian
Series Designer: Adam Mietlowski

Photo Research by Anne Burns Images
Cover Photo by Science Photo Library: Eric Nguyen/Jim Reed Photography

The photographs in this book are used with permission and through the courtesy of: *Peter Arnold*: p. 1, 32 Gene Rhoden; p. 4, 23 Weatherstock. *AP/Wide World Photos*: p. 7, 39, 40, 43. *Photo Researchers, Inc.*: p. 8 Katherine Bay/Jim Reed Photography; p. 12, 31 Jim Reed; p. 36 Mike Berger/Jim Reed Photography. *NOAA*: p. 11, 20, 28 National Severe Storms Laboratory; p. 19 NOAA; p. 24 NWS/Forecast Offices and River Forecast Centers. *Photofest*: p. 15. *Getty Images*: p. 16 National Geographic. *Science Photo Library*: p. 35 Reed Timmer and Jim Bishop/Jim Reed Photography.

Printed in Malaysia

6 5 4 3 2 1

Contents

Path of Destruction   5

Tornadoes Defined   10

The Life Cycle of a Tornado   21

The Tornado Intensity Scale   25

Forecasting Tornadoes   26

Keep Yourself Safe   38

Glossary   44

Find Out More   46

Index   48

Path of Destruction

A towering *thunderstorm* moves across the Oklahoma countryside. *Hail* crashes down onto fields of crops. As the hail passes, a rotating *wall cloud* drops from the base of the storm. Below it, dust begins to swirl up from the ground.

Dust swirls beneath an ominous wall cloud near Adrian, Texas.

Moments later, a tornado appears. With the roar of one hundred freight trains, the *twister* bears down on an isolated farm. Trees snap like twigs. Loose boards turn into missiles. A pickup truck flies into the air and crashes to the ground a hundred yards away. The *vortex* hits the farmhouse and the building seems to explode, torn apart in an instant by the force of the whirling winds.

Then, as swiftly as it came, the tornado moves on, leaving toys, dolls, books, and bits of furniture spread across the open fields.

A man wipes his eyes after searching for survivors from a 1999 tornado in Louisiana. The dog is part of the search team.

Very few people have ever seen the inside of a tornado and lived to tell about it. On June 16, 1928, a man named Will Keller did just that. As a twister approached his Kansas farm, Keller saw the funnel lift off the ground and move slowly over his head. Here is what he reported to the local newspaper:

There was a strong, gassy odor . . . a screaming, hissing sound . . . I looked up . . . There was a circular opening in the center of the funnel . . . The walls of this opening were of rotating clouds and the whole was made brilliantly visible by constant flashes of lightning which zigzagged from side to side.

Frightening and deadly, tornadoes are a fascinating natural phenomenon—and very difficult to study.

◀ *A tornado whirls across a dirt road in front of a Kansas state trooper. The image was created by overlapping a photograph and a video frame.*

Tornadoes Defined

A tornado is a violently rotating column of air extending between a thunderstorm cloud and the ground. As the air turns at speeds of up to 300 miles per hour (483 kilometers per hour), it also rises rapidly, sometimes at more than 100 mph (98 kph). The spiraling action continues high into the clouds overhead, sometimes reaching several miles into the atmosphere.

A tornado photographed near Anadarko, Oklahoma, in May 1999. This same storm later formed into an F5 tornado that hit Oklahoma City.

Tornadoes develop during severe thunderstorms, but only about one percent of thunderstorms actually spawn tornadoes. They form during any month of the year and at any time of day. On November 6, 2005, a fierce tornado struck parts of Indiana and Kentucky at 2 AM, while many residents were asleep. As a result, the tornado killed twenty-two people. However, most tornadoes hit in the spring and summer months, between 3 PM and 9 PM. Tornadoes occur all over the world, with the highest number in the United States.

Tornadoes rarely move in a straight line. Some move very slowly or hardly at all. The average twister tracks across the ground at about 35 mph (56 kph). Most tornadoes are less than 150 yards (137 meters) wide but some are much, much wider. On May 31, 1985, for example, one measuring 2.2 miles (3.5 km) wide cut through an uninhabited area of Pennsylvania.

◀ *A powerful thunderstorm approaches a farm in northern Nebraska.*

Most tornadoes are on the ground for less than half an hour, but the Great Tri-State Tornado of 1925 lasted for three hours and twenty-nine minutes and covered 217 miles (215 km) through Missouri, Illinois, and Indiana. It also killed the most people—695—of any tornado in the United States.

On average, fewer than one hundred people die from tornadoes each year in the United States. The most violent 2 percent of storms cause 70 percent of the fatalities. The deadliest twister in history struck the South Asian nation of Bangladesh in 1989. It claimed about 1,300 lives and injured 12,000 people, in addition to leaving about 80,000 homeless.

Tornadoes can be terrifying, as this image from the movie Twister *(1996) shows.*

Some of the most damaging effects of a tornado come from small tornadoes that sometimes form within the walls of the main funnel. These *suction vortices* (singular: suction vortex) last only a short time—a few seconds or minutes—but their winds are particularly fierce. Suction vortices usually hide in the dust clouds that surround the storm, making them hard to see. Because a suction vortex is small, it can utterly destroy one house but leave a house ten feet away undamaged.

◄ *This tornado destroyed Manchester, South Dakota, just minutes before the tornado was photographed.*

Tornadoes are not the only kinds of swirling winds our planet experiences. Dust devils, which in rare cases can be strong enough to flip a car, are often seen swirling across open ground or parking lots. They form when the heated ground causes hot air to rise in a strong *updraft*.

Waterspouts are tornadoes that form over water. Although waterspouts appear to be sucking up water out of the ocean, the swirling column is actually filled with droplets condensing out of the moist air, not droplets lifted from the water below. If a waterspout crosses onto dry land, it is then considered a regular tornado, and can be just as dangerous.

This waterspout was photographed from an aircraft off the Florida Keys. ▶

The Life Cycle of a Tornado

Despite decades of research, *meteorologists* still do not know exactly how tornadoes develop. This may seem surprising, but tornadoes are hard to study: they're rare, short-lived, and dangerous. Only once or twice a year do scientists get a chance to study a storm.

In 1973, *storm chasers* from the National Severe Storms Laboratory (NSSL) and the University of Oklahoma surrounded a tornado and documented its five stages. In Stage 1, the dust whirl stage, dust whirls on the ground and a short funnel hangs down from the cloud overhead. The two parts do not look connected, but they are. In Stage 2, the organizing stage, the vortex becomes visible and is usually light colored. The funnel will then darken as dust and debris get swept up into it.

This is the first tornado ever captured by storm chasers from the National Severe Storms Laboratory. It is shown here in an early stage.

In Stage 3, the mature stage, the tornado is almost vertical and is at its most damaging stage. Some stay mature for only a few minutes, but others stay in this stage for more than an hour. In Stage 4, the shrinking stage, the tornado thins and the column tilts to one side. As the tornado narrows, the winds usually get faster, so this stage can still be very dangerous. During Stage 5, the decaying or rope stage, cool air from the surrounding thunderstorm interferes with the tornado. The tornado stretches out into a ropelike shape before disappearing completely.

The whole process of tornado formation takes only seconds or up to several hours, depending on the conditions. Sometimes storms will skip stages. Sometimes a decaying tornado gets wrapped up in a new tornado, or "tornado family." Some scientists think the Great Tri-State Tornado of 1925 was actually a tornado family of two or more tornadoes.

A decaying tornado in the rope stage.

F-Scale Number	Wind Speed (miles per hour)	Damage Description	Frequency Average
F0	40–72	Some damage to chimneys or TV antennas; breaks branches off trees; pushes over trees with shallow roots; old trees with hollow insides break or fall; signs and billboards damaged.	29%
F1	73–112	Peels off roofs; windows broken; mobile homes pushed or overturned; trees on soft ground uprooted; some trees snapped; moving vehicles pushed off roads.	40%
F2	113–157	Roofs torn off frame houses leaving strong upright walls standing; weak structures or outbuildings demolished; railroad cars pushed over; large trees snapped or uprooted; light objects become flying debris; cars blown off highway.	24%
F3	158–206	Roofs and some walls torn off well-constructed frame houses; some rural buildings completely demolished or flattened; trains overturned; steel-framed structures torn; cars lifted off the ground and may roll some distance; most trees in a forest uprooted, snapped, or leveled.	6%
F4	207–260	Well-constructed frame houses leveled; structures with weak foundations lifted, torn, and blown off some distance; bark ripped off trees by small flying debris; sandy soil eroded and gravel flies in high winds; cars thrown or rolled a considerable distance; large objects become flying debris.	2%
F5	261–318	Strong frame houses lifted clear off foundation and carried a considerable distance and destroyed; steel-reinforced concrete structures badly damaged; trees completely stripped of their bark; incredible phenomena can occur.	less than 1%
F6	319–sonic	Extent and types of damage too great to be imagined.	0%

The Tornado Intensity Scale

Researchers classify tornadoes on a scale called the "Fujita-Pearson Scale of Tornado Intensity," developed by Ted Fujita in 1971. Experts survey the damage caused by the storm and give it a rating from F0 to F5, based on the single most destructive thing the storm does. If the worst damage consists of broken tree limbs and mangled TV antennas, the tornado gets an F0 rating. In this kind of storm, the winds do not get higher than 72 mph (116 kph). At the extreme end of the scale, an F5 tornado has winds of up to 318 mph (512 kph) and can completely destroy strong frame houses, leaving only the concrete foundations behind. Usually only one storm per year gets the F5 rating.

◀ *The Fujita-Pearson Scale of Tornado Intensity. Scientists review the damage before rating the storm.*

Forecasting Tornadoes

For most of the nineteenth and twentieth centuries, there were no tornado forecasts. In fact, the word "tornado" was banned from all public weather forecasts from 1887 to 1952 because officials thought people would either panic or ignore the warnings.

By the 1950s, scientists recognized that certain weather patterns over the Great Plains seemed to lead to tornadoes in the area known as *Tornado Alley*. When warm, wet air from the Caribbean; dry air from Mexico; and a high level of cold, dry air from Canada all collided, trouble often followed.

Experts disagree over the exact boundaries of "Tornado Alley," but much of the United States is vulnerable to tornadoes.

Tornado Alley

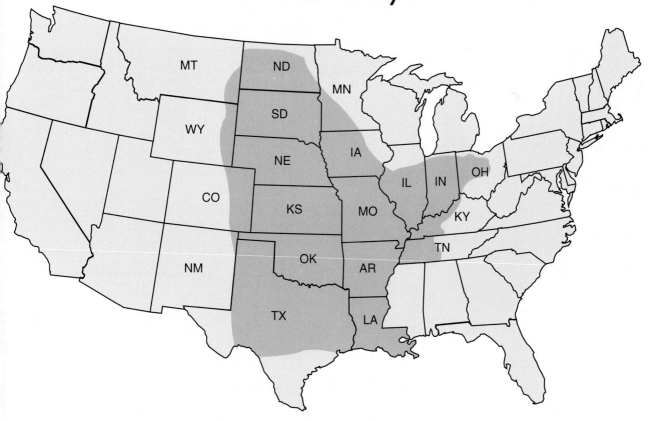

In the 1970s, forecasts became more accurate as researchers learned more about *supercell thunderstorms*, which generate the fiercest tornadoes. An ordinary thunderstorm consists of one or more "cells," each of which contains an updraft of warm air and a *downdraft* of cold air. Supercell thunderstorms have updrafts that are many times stronger than in an average storm. Supercell updrafts can reach up to 150 mph (241 kph). Supercell storms can extend 10 miles (16 km) through the atmosphere, towering more than 50,000 feet (15,240 m) from top to bottom. Their intense updrafts and downdrafts often cause heavy rain and hail along with strong winds at ground level.

Hail from a severe thunderstorm covers roads and grass. The largest hailstones pictured are about 2 to 3 inches (5–7.6 cm) in diameter.

Forecasters can tell which supercells are particularly dangerous by looking into them with *Doppler radar*. If the Doppler radar reveals a *mesocyclone*—a swirling column of air several miles above ground and sometimes several miles in diameter—forecasters know conditions are ripe for tornado formation. They get another hint if they see a *Tornadic Vortex Signature*. This is a narrower area of particularly intense rotation, and it is sometimes visible up to half an hour before a tornado strikes. Still, supercell thunderstorms with mesocyclones spawn tornadoes only about half the time. And some storms without mesocyclones create quick-forming and dangerous twisters.

This Doppler on Wheels (DOW) scans for tornadoes during a Kansas thunderstorm.

Over time, different theories have been proposed for tornado formation. The discovery of mesocyclones and Tornadic Vortex Signatures with Doppler radar led many scientists to think that tornadoes formed high up in the supercell thunderstorm and then extended downward to the ground.

A wall cloud develops during a severe thunderstorm in western Oklahoma.

Current research, though, suggests that the process might be more complex and that tornadoes might actually start close to or on the ground. Tornadoes often develop at the place where two strong downdrafts—one on the front *flank* of the storm and one on the rear flank—come together. Unfortunately, the area between 10 and 300 feet (3–91 m) from ground level—where these winds interact—is the hardest to study with today's meteorological equipment.

When the mystery of tornado formation is solved, forecasters might be able to make better predictions of where and when tornadoes will strike.

The tornado in this photo is moving away from the photographer, but the major patterns of air movement around the vortex can still be seen.

Rear Flank
Downdraft (RFD)

Updraft

Funnel/Vortex

Forward Flank
Downdraft (FFD)

Debris Cloud

Despite these uncertainties, people are usually given at least some warning that a tornado is coming their way. The National Weather Service provides three levels of forecasts. The first, a "severe weather outlook," can cover several states, and means that severe storms might develop. The next level, a "tornado watch," means that dangerous storms have developed. A watch usually covers several counties or part of a state. A "tornado warning" is much more serious. It means a tornado is about to happen or one has already been spotted on the ground. You should seek shelter immediately if a warning is issued.

A tornado moves across a South Dakota street as storm chasers hurry to capture it on film.

Keep Yourself Safe

Have a disaster plan for you and your family, and make sure your school has one, too. The American Red Cross can provide information to help you.

Stay informed about storms by listening for tornado watches and warnings on the radio and on television. If a tornado warning is issued, move to a safe place right away.

If there are no tornado shelters nearby, go to the basement. If there is no basement, move to an interior room or hallway on the lowest level of the building you are in and try to get under a sturdy piece of furniture. If you're outside, lie flat in a ditch or other low spot, if possible, and protect your head.

Students take cover during a tornado drill.

Taking shelter under a highway overpass is *not* a good idea. The overpass can actually make the tornado's winds more damaging. Plus, people who do this might block the way for emergency vehicles.

Mobile homes are among the most dangerous places to be when a tornado hits because they are easily torn apart. You are much safer in a stronger building or shelter. Automobiles are also dangerous places to be during a tornado, particularly if you're trying to outrun a storm that is bearing down on you. However, a 2002 study by researchers at Kent State University in Ohio showed that a parked car might actually be safer than a mobile home.

◀ *Here we see tornado damage to a mobile home park in Louisiana in April 1999.*

Every tornado is unique, so use your best judgment to keep yourself safe. Before a storm hits, think about safe places for shelter in your home and school. Talk with adults about how to protect yourself if a tornado were to strike.

This storm shelter was the only part of the house left intact after a tornado tore through this home near Lyndon, Kansas, in May 2003. Luckily, the owners were away when the tornado struck.

Glossary

Doppler radar—A radar system for determining the speed of a moving object.

downdraft—An area where air is moving downward.

flank—The side of any object.

hail—Showers of small pellets or balls of ice falling from cumulonimbus, or vertically shaped, clouds.

mesocyclone—A rotating column of air inside a thunderstorm.

meteorologists—Scientists who study the atmosphere, including the weather and the climate.

storm chasers—People who try to observe tornadoes at close range, either for scientific study or for thrills.

suction vortices—Small, violent tornadoes that form in the walls of the main tornado.

supercell thunderstorm—A very powerful thunderstorm that can rise 10 miles (16 km) into the atmosphere.

thunderstorm—A storm of lightning and thunder, usually with rain and gusty winds.

Tornadic Vortex Signature—A pattern of intense air rotation within a supercell thunderstorm, visible on Doppler radar.

Tornado Alley—An area of the midwestern and southern United States that has the highest numbers of tornadoes in the world. The states of Texas, Oklahoma, Kansas, Nebraska, and Iowa make up the "alley."

twister—A slang term for a tornado.

updraft—An area where air is moving upward.

vortex—A whirling mass of air or water. The plural form of this word is *vortices*.

wall cloud—A dark cloud that appears under the base of a thunderstorm as a tornado is forming. The tornado forms underneath the wall cloud.

Find Out More

Books

Elsom, Derek. *Weather Explained: A Beginner's Guide to the Elements.*
New York: Henry Holt, 1997.

Pratt Nicolson, Cynthia. *Tornado.* Toronto: Kids Can Press, 2003.

Simon, Seymour. *Tornadoes.* New York: Morrow Junior Books, 1999.

White, Matt. *Storm Chasers: On the Trail of Deadly Tornadoes.*
Mankato, MN: Capstone, 2003.

Web Sites

National Weather Service / National Oceanic & Atmospheric
Administration
http://www.education.noaa.gov/
http://www.nws.noaa.gov/om/brochures/tornado.shtml
http://www.nws.noaa.gov/om/reachout/tornadoes.shtml

Other Tornado Sites
http://www.tornadoproject.com/
http://www.ucar.edu/educ_outreach/webweather/
http://weatherwizkids.com/tornado.htm

About the Author

Joe Thoron is a freelance writer in Washington state. When not writing for children, he builds Web sites and writes marketing copy. He lives on an island north of Seattle, right between several sleeping volcanoes and a major earthquake zone.

Index

Page numbers for illustrations are in **boldface**.

Bangladesh, 14

classification, **24**, 25
conditions, 26, 30

damage, 6, **7**, 14–17, **24**, 25, **40**, **43**
deaths, 13, 14
debris cloud, **35**
dogs, **7**
Doppler on Wheels, **31**
Doppler radar, 30, 31, 33
downdrafts, 29, 34, **35**
duration, 6, 14, 17, 22
dust, **4**, 5, 17, **21**
dust devils, 18

forecasting, 26–37, **31**
formation, **20**, 21–22, **23**, 26, 33–34, **35**
Fujita-Pearson Scale, **24**, 25

geographic areas, 13, 26, **27**, 37

Great Tri-State Tornado of 1925, 14, 22

hail, 5, **28**, 29

inside view, 9

lightning, 9

mesocyclones, 30, 33
mobile homes, 24, **40**, 41
movement, 13, 14
movies, **15**

odor, 9

rain, 29
rotation, 9, 10, 18, 30

safety, 37–42, **39**, **43**
seasons, 13
severe weather outlook, 37
shape, 21, 22
sizes, 13, 17, 29
sounds, 6, 9
speeds, 10, 13, 22, 29
stages, 21–22, **23**

storm chasers, 9, **20**, 21, **31**, **36**
suction vortices, 17
survivors, **7**, 9

thunderstorms, 5, **12**, 13, 29, **32**
supercell, 29–30, 33
Tornadic Vortex Signature, 30
Tornado Alley, 26, **27**
tornadoes, defined, 10, **35**
tornado family, 22

updrafts, 18, 29, **35**

vortex, 6, 21

wall cloud, **4**, 5, **32**, **35**
warning, 37
watch, 37
water spouts, 18, **19**
winds, 6, 24, 25, 29, 34, 41